The Pig
ROBERT P

CHRIS SWINNEY

CRIMES CANADA
TRUE CRIMES THAT
SHOCKED THE NATION VOL. 1

TRUE CRIMES THAT SHOCKED
THE NATION

ROBERT PICKTON
Volume I

by **Chris Swinney**

A Crimes Canada
True Crimes That Shocked The
Nation eBook

ISBN-13: **978-1508505341**
ISBN-10: **1508505349**
Published by:

Vronsky Parker Publication
an Imprint of
RJ Parker Publishing, Inc.

Published in Canada

Crimes Canada: True Crimes That Shocked the Nation

Series Introduction

Canadians take pride in their reputation as a "nice" and "polite" people, as global blue-helmeted United Nations peacekeepers. Canadians often like to point to their American neighbours and the reported high crimes rates remarking on just how safe Canadian cities are.

Canada's largest city, Toronto, with a population of 2.8 million people had only 57 homicides in 2014, while Chicago with 2.7 million people reported 425 murders in the same year. Canadians will tell you that nobody in Canada has a "constitutional right to bear arms" and that no firearm, handgun or rifle, can be purchased without the buyer first being checked by the local police and issued a Firearms Acquisition Certificate (FAC).

Handguns are very difficult to acquire legally, and a permit to actually carry one beyond driving with it unloaded and locked in the trunk of your car to and from a gun range, is almost impossible.   Until recently, by law, rifles had to be registered with a national gun registry, and automatic and many military grade semi-automatic rifles, and high capacity magazines are completely outlawed.   Canada has a relatively good reputation for peaceful race relations and unlike the United States which has taken the "melting pot" approach to immigration, Canada celebrates and encourages "multiculturalism."   Urban "ghettos," although they exist in Canada, are few and far in between.

But having said all that, when Canadians go off the rails and perpetrate a violent crime, it is often so spectacularly crazy that it makes headlines around the world.   From the mysterious still unsolved disappearance in 1919 in Toronto of Canadian millionaire Ambrose Small that was dubbed in the international press as a "crime of the century" in its time, to the recent world-wide coverage of gay porn actor Luka Magnotta's murder and necrophiliac dismemberment of a victim recorded on videotape and posted on social media, Canada's crimes often not only shock the nation, but the world too.

Canadians who might be smug about their sense of security and safety and sense of order forget that some of the world's most shocking crimes took place in Canada. Cases like:

- Serial killer Clifford Olsen who murdered 11 children and then persuaded authorities to pay his family $10,000 for every body whose burial site he would reveal;

- The husband and wife serial killers known as "Ken & Barbie"—Paul Bernardo and Karla Homolka—who kidnapped, raped, tortured and killed adolescent girls, videotaping their horrific crimes along the way, including the rape and death of Karla's own kid sister;

- Mark Twitchell--the "Dexter Killer"--a wannabe filmmaker and fan of the Dexter TV show who set up his own murder studio in a laneway garage and used the internet to lure a victim to it, murdering and dismembering him;

- Mark Lepine, a crazed mass murderer who in a fit of rage entered an engineering college, separated the male students from the females, and murdered 14 women before committing suicide;

- The Quebec Biker War between the Hells Angels and the Rock Machine outlaw motorcycle clubs that claimed 150 lives;

- Canada's Mafia Wars that took 35 victims in 2012 alone between warring mobsters in Toronto and Montreal;

- The rape-murder of a street shoeshine boy by a ring of pedophiles on Toronto's then notorious Yonge Street "strip";

- Russell Williams, a colonel in the Canadian Air Force and a commander of a strategic airbase, who piloted the Queen of England, Price Philip and the Prime Minister of Canada, and was convicted of raping, torturing and murdering two women while videotaping his crimes;

- Peter Woodcock who murdered three children by the time he was seventeen, was confined to a psychiatric facility for thirty-four years until the day he was given his first day pass, when he murdered a fourth victim;

- And the subject of this volume, Robert Pickton, a British Columbia man who inherited a pig farm worth a million dollars and used his wealth to lure skid row hookers to his farm where he confessed to murdering 49 female victims, dismembering them and feeding their body parts to his pigs which he supplied to Vancouver area restaurants.

In this multi-volume series edited by crime historian Dr. Peter Vronsky and true crime author and publisher RJ Parker, some of Canada's most notorious shocking crimes will be described and explored, including some of the cases mentioned above.

Crimes Canada: True Crimes that Shocked the Nation, will feature a series of Canadian true crime books published by VP Publication (Vronsky & Parker), an imprint of **RJ Parker Publishing, Inc.**, one of the world's leading Indie publishers of true crime.

Peter Vronsky is the bestselling author of *Serial Killers: The Method and Madness of Monsters* and *Female Serial Killers: How and Why Women Become Monsters* while R.J. Parker is not only a successful Indie publisher but also the author of books like *Serial Killers*

Abridged: An Encyclopedia of 100 Serial Killers, *Social Media Monsters: Internet Killers Parents Who Killed Their Children: Filicide*, and *Serial Killer Groupies*. Both are Canadians and have teamed up to share shocking Canadian true crime cases not only with fellow Canadian readers but with Americans and world readers as well, who will be shocked and horrified by just how evil and sick "nice" Canadians can be when they go bad.

Finally, the editors invite their established Canadian fellow authors and aspiring authors to submit proposals or manuscripts to VP Publication at Agent@RJParkerPublishing.com.

VP Publication is a new frontier Indie publisher, offering their published authors a generous royalty agreement payable within three months of publishing and aggressive online marketing support. Unlike many so-called "publishers" that are nothing but vanity presses in disguise, VP Publication does not charge authors in advance for submitting their proposal or manuscripts, nor do we charge authors if we choose to publish their works. We pay you, and pay well.

Robert William "Willie" Pickton

Illustration 1: The Pig Farmer Killer

Robert William "Willie" Pickton was born in Port Coquitlam, British Columbia, Canada on October 24, 1949 to Louise Pickton Wright and Leonard Pickton. By all accounts, he was raised primarily by his mother. However, family friends, and later Robert himself, would explain that his father was around just long enough to brutally beat him when he was in trouble. Beyond the known beatings, the relationship between Robert and his father is left up to one's imagination and little is known about it. The man was clearly in the picture, but he was the parent who would dole out punishment and didn't get involved with his children's lives. Louise became the primary caregiver for the Pickton children, but she was far from nurturing. Most of my research indicated she never had time for the children because she ran a successful meat company which required long hours. Whatever the case was, she'd end up teaching them little about being contributing members in society, and much about pigs and the tough life one lives when raising and butchering them.

Regardless of whom you choose to believe actually raised Robert and his brother, David Francis Pickton, or his sister, Linda Louise Wright, it was clear the environment was unhealthy during the time this case took shape, and downright filthy compared to today's standards. Based on my research, it was clear Robert Pickton did not have a normal childhood. As mentioned, the family owned a meat business that was profitable, but required long hours and dirty jobs to keep the place running. Even while in grade school, Louise demanded Robert and his siblings work on the farm, slopping pigs and taking care of the other animals instead of focusing on school work or playing with the few friends they had. The farm was the bread and butter for the Pickton Family, and nothing would get in the way of the needs of the farm.

It has been well documented that Robert would remain quiet for long periods of time, and I suspect it was because he would internalize all that he saw or that happened to him while on the farm. He liked to hide when he was in trouble, like when he knew he was going to catch a beating from his father, and over the years he needed to come up with new spots because his parents knew where to look. A story told by a childhood friend, yet never confirmed by Robert himself, suggested Robert would hide by crawling into the gutted carcass of a large hog when he really messed up. Whether that's true or not, we might not ever know, but it's disturbing to say the least.[1]

The family farm, good, bad, or indifferent, ended up being the only place Robert would ever know. It's hard while writing this imagining anything good or fun happening for him, or his siblings, while at the farm. Eventually, the farm proved to be the place that would cause Robert much grief and turmoil. However, many other people would suffer and ultimately be murdered because of the same farm. The place Robert called home would haunt him, and the things he saw or did while he was there would lead to many sad days for him while growing up.

In various interviews,[11] Robert would be asked about, or voluntarily talk about, what he considered "normal" to be. In these discussions, when he tried to reflect on what "normal" meant to him, he talked about a calf being born on the farm that he became fond of.

He said, while thinking back to his childhood, *I'm gonna keep this calf for the rest of my life. Then I came back from school two weeks later – the calf was gone. I says around the house, 'Where's my calf?'"*

"They say, 'Maybe you should take a walk down the barn.' I said, 'no, no way. They kill animals down there.'"

Robert went down to the barn, "Anyway, there's my calf, upside down, cleaned out, butchered. I couldn't talk to anybody for about four days."

He was partial to the calf, and the incident rocked him pretty badly. He was so traumatized by the incident, even into adulthood, that it became something he'd only share with people he was close to (or when asked about it) and something I believe he never truly dealt with internally.

Schooling was difficult for Robert for many reasons. He was considered "slow" and required special education classes. Being in the "special" classes wore on him and was embarrassing. Some believe he may have had a learning disability, but he was never tested (there weren't many options during this time anyway) and consequently fell further behind each year. He'd eventually drop out halfway through high school as the frustration and constant teasing from his peers proved too much for him to handle. Unlike what your or my parents would have likely done if we dropped out, there was no fallout by Robert's parents about his decision to do so. In fact, Louise saw an opportunity to order Robert around the farm almost twenty-four hours a day. He spent nearly every minute of every day working on the farm. I think I would have run away at some point, but Robert was born into the situation and likely had no idea the grass might be greener on the other side.

Robert seemed to get along with his brother and sister okay. He would later tell investigators that his sister never liked the farm and tried to be away from it as much as possible. His brother, on the other hand, followed Robert around the farm, and they worked together often. The Pickton children went through difficult times together, and they stuck together. Robert was close with his siblings because the truth of the matter was, he wasn't able to make many friends and he never dated.

We already know that he was quiet, "slow," and dropped out of school, but the lack of friends was largely due to the fact that his personal hygiene was deplorable. He stunk of dead animals, pigs, and manure, and his hair and clothes were unkempt, causing girls to avoid him like a plague. People constantly made fun of him, but he was comfortable with himself. According to his own admission, Robert was mortified of showers and said it was because his mother forced him to take them when he was young.

One of his friends, a woman he called "The Nag," would occasionally convince him that he stank so bad that he needed to take a bath. If he didn't clean himself up, she threatened to stop hanging around him. Robert would begrudgingly oblige, but he'd still come out smelling unsavory. His whole life was spent around dead animals, death, slop, and manure. His skin was similar to that of the pigs he raised and slaughtered-leathery and putrid. However, the same environment that caused people to shun him was where he found salvation, felt safe like you and I do in our own homes and despite his tough mother and the beatings from his father, he was marginally safe. Psychologically, it seems he familiarized himself with the smell of the pigs and from hiding in their carcasses as a "safe" place. Therefore, showering could likely bring him back to why he was hiding and remind him of when his mother would force him to shower afterward.

Robert Pickton did not have a place as a child to release his anger, and he did not possess the social skills to release any sexual desires in other ways. He grew up being taught that it was healthy to slaughter many animals. As previously mentioned, I firmly believe the environment he grew up in completely contributed to what was to come.

A childhood story worth sharing, and one that demonstrates the environment Robert Pickton was raised in, involved his younger brother, David, and his mother. David had just obtained his driver's license and had taken his father's red truck (painted with red house paint to save money) for a ride into town. Along the way, he managed to run over Tim Barrett, a 14-year-old boy who lived nearby. David freaked out, jumped out of the truck, and rushed over to Tim. He saw Tim was mangled and seriously wounded. He immediately reported what had happened to his mother. Louise arrived at the scene (it's unclear if she walked there or David drove her there) looked over Tim, and apparently decided there was nothing that could be done for him. She bent over, pushed, and rolled Tim to the edge of the road. Below the road down an embankment was a deep slough that paralleled the road. Without hesitation, Louise pushed Tim into the slough, turned around, and calmly walked back to the farm to get back to work.

David observed his mother's actions and determined he needed to do something to protect himself. He drove the red truck into town and met a man who serviced his family's vehicles. David convinced the mechanic to fix the dented bumper and replace the front turn light, but the mechanic refused to re-paint the truck. There was no reason provided as to why the mechanic wouldn't re-paint the truck.

While this incident was unfolding, the boy's parents frantically called neighbors looking for their son because it was very unlike him not to report his whereabouts to his parents. Eventually, Tim's father set out to search for his son. He checked neighboring farms, made numerous phone calls, and still could not find his son. Finally, while walking along the road where neighbors reported they saw his son last (which was also the way back to his house), Tim's father discovered a shoe on the road that he knew his son was wearing that day. But, when he checked the road and brush for his son, he was nowhere to be seen. His father looked over the edge into the slough and saw every parent's worst nightmare...Tim was floating lifeless in the murky slough water. As quickly as he could,

Tim's father called the police, who responded right away.

Tim was later fished from the slough. An autopsy was conducted and indicated Tim died from drowning; however, it was noted that he had a fractured skull with sub-cranial hemorrhage and a fractured and dislocated pelvis. The pathologist who conducted the autopsy stated the injuries would not have killed Tim. Therefore, had David, or his mother Louise, done the right thing and called for help, Tim would have likely survived.

A year later, an informal hearing (much of it hearsay, but some accounts by the mechanic who repaired the red truck and the original police officer who responded to the initial report were heard) regarding Tim's death was held. For an unknown reason, Tim's death was ruled accidental; however, David had a juvenile proceeding as a result (which is sealed and one could only speculate as to what occurred in such a hearing), and Louise Pickton was never charged. Although this incident involved David, you can bet Robert knew about it and learned from his mother that human life, unless it was their own, did not matter. It also had a resounding effect on the kids. If they didn't know already prior to this incident, it was clear now, their mother should be feared.

Despite everything we know about Robert's mother and how brutal she was, Robert remained closest with her instead of his father. Based on how she treated him, it's unclear why, but it makes you wonder just how bad his father was. Anyway, Louise was eccentric, possibly psychotic, but at the same time, she was the one parent that Robert could rely upon. Many who have followed this case believe she, in her own sick and twisted way, taught Robert and his siblings how to run the farm through "tough love" and provided them both the male and female role model they needed while growing up.

The Pickton Family continued to live like this for many years and kept mostly to themselves. They had contacts and friends who would sell their meat for them. Neighbors also ate meat from their farm. However, as time slipped by, Louise developed cancer. She fought it for four years, but eventually, she passed away in 1976. A short time later, Leonard too passed away (late 1970's). This left Robert and his siblings to run a busy meat farm by themselves, tend to the animals, and try to pay bills.

The siblings struggled to keep the farm going but managed to stay afloat...for a while. After a few years, the work became too much, and they decided to only keep enough pigs to slaughter to provide local neighbors with meat. This did not pay the farm's mounting bills, though. In 1994 and 1995, pieces of the land were sold for approximately $5.16 million.[2] This large amount of money contributed to sweeping changes in Robert's and his siblings' lives. They had always had hand-me-down clothing, little food (besides pork), no toys, beat-up vehicles, then boom, overnight, they became millionaires. Although Robert was still quiet and did not drink alcohol or use drugs at this time, his sister and younger brother took a liking to the new-found wealth and began throwing parties at the farm and making "friends." They were no longer misfits and were popular now (unfortunately, all due to the money).

Robert and his siblings continued with changes, starting with naming the remaining piece of property "Piggy Palace," and before long, if you were into sex, drugs, and alcohol, you partied at Piggy Palace. Robert fancied himself as a businessman and created a non-profit "society" that he named, "Piggy Palace Good Times Society." Events at the Palace drew over a thousand party-goers at a time. The Picktons were finally living high on the hog. However, local authorities began receiving numerous complaints from neighbors that drugs, alcohol, and sex were rampant during these parties and reported hearing female screams all through the night. It was also alleged that underage females were being forced to have sex with adult men on the farm, but the police did not investigate these reports initially. In fact, it would take months of complaints before they would finally investigate Piggy Palace.

Illustration 2: Dozens of aboriginal sex trade workers were slaughtered at 'Piggy Palace'

After numerous visits from the police and several attempts to get the Picktons to limit or control the activity at Piggy Palace, relations between the Picktons and the Vancouver Police Department (VPD) began to deteriorate.

On December 31, 1998, a massive New Year's party was thrown at Piggy Palace. It was described as an all-out deviant foray. People passed out on the property, on the roads near the property, and were stopped leaving the farm heavily intoxicated. Shortly thereafter, Robert was served an injunction banning any and all future parties on the farm. The court order read that police were "henceforth, authorized to arrest and remove any person attending public events at the farm." The court order, and the fact Robert failed to provide mandatory financial statements, led to the nonprofit status of the "Society" being removed in January of 2000.

Even after being warned, served an order to cease, and heavy law enforcement presence in the area, the parties continued. VPD, as most agencies will do when someone pisses them off, decided to make Piggy Palace a small project. They were intent on shutting down all the parties and illegal activity. While working the property, officers began seeing Robert, on numerous occasions, heading to Vancouver's Downtown Eastside (Low Track) and picking up prostitutes to bring back to the farm. Neighbors described the Pickton Family as bizarre, and while VPD was looking for ways to lessen the illegal activity at the farm, the neighbors were calling regularly to report suspicious activity and alleged the Picktons were out of control.

The fact Robert and his brother were being seen bringing so many prostitutes to the farm caused the Vancouver Police Department to believe another, and much larger problem in Vancouver, could have ties to the Picktons.

In September of 1998, the Vancouver Police Department began an investigative Task Force to help locate a growing list of missing prostitutes from the Low Track area. The investigation would stretch for years, solicit international attention, and cost the crown millions of dollars. But, the families and friends of the almost one-hundred missing women (in 1998) wanted answers and demanded the police department get involved. Unfortunately, the investigation would reveal a disturbing and dark secret that no one involved was prepared for.

Vancouver's Downtown Eastside, aka "Low Track," earned its reputation in the 1970's (which sadly it still maintains today) as one of the vilest locations in North America, beating out similar seedy locales found in Chicago, Detroit, and East Los Angeles. Among the list of offenses garnishing such a demoralizing title are underage prostitution (some girls starting at age 11), turf wars by drug lords and cartels ending up in regular shootings and stabbings, rampant overdoses leading to several deaths, and a staggering statistic indicating one-fourth of its residents are HIV positive,-but these unsavory facts, each disturbing and unbelievable in its own right, would become minimal compared to what was happening behind closed doors in Low Track. A person was preying on women and had done so for two decades, under the noses of the police, and would continue to do so until being caught.

During my career, I've been to the worst of the worst in the San Francisco Bay Area, including homicide scenes in roach-infested sheds and dead body calls where the skin drips off the deceased, but the accounts and descriptions provided by women who lived and "worked" in Low Track made me shudder. Suddenly the mean streets of Oakland, East Palo Alto, Richmond, and San Jose didn't seem so bad.

Although men were murdered in the rough-and-tumble streets of Low Track, women had things exponentially worse. Since the mid 1970's, hundreds of women have gone "missing" after setting foot in the modern-day wasteland, and equal numbers have been abused, physically and sexually, by johns and their pimps.[3] A sub-culture of death, overdose, and sexual perversion cluttered the streets with lost souls. Compounding the madness was the fact all of this illegal activity was snubbed by the Vancouver Police Department (VPD) and later, the Royal Canadian Mounted Police (RCMP). Most of these egregious actions occurred right under their noses. This fact continues to make families who have a member on the "Missing Women List" angry, and they continue to want to know why it was allowed to get that bad, and why so many of the women still haven't been found.

Were it not for continual reporting by family members and friends that their loved ones were missing, this case could have gone on even longer. Still, the Vancouver Police Department dismissed the reports because the women being reported as missing were also prostitutes. VPD believed prostitutes lived "transient" lifestyles and could have left Low Track to "work" somewhere else. VPD also pointed out that no one ever cooperated with their investigations. Pimps and drug pushers never talked to the police, and the hookers knew not to either, or end up beaten or dead. This is the kind of stuff that gives police officers a bad reputation.

As I dove into this case, the hair on the back of my neck began to stand straight up. One of my hopes for this project is that by bringing awareness to the events that unfolded at Low Track, we as a society will not commit the same mistakes or make the same terrible decisions that without a doubt cost many women their lives.

Women, and later female children, of all ages, types, and sizes began "officially" disappearing in 1983, although records indicate the first missing woman was reported in 1971. However, as mentioned above, it wasn't until September of 1998 (15 years later!) that anyone, specifically Detective Dave Dickson, decided to look into numerous reports of missing women, all of whom were known prostitutes.

Almost immediately after Dickson started talking to people and other investigators about the case, it became a strong possibility in his eyes, and others', that a serial killer may be preying on prostitutes in the Low Track area. VPD did not want to alarm the community and therefore kept this concern under wraps, but after a while, it seemed obvious that female prostitutes were being targeted. But there were no bodies being discovered. Investigators, going on their own preconceived notions about how prostitutes lived, assumed these women were "in transit" and noted they normally do not maintain services, utilities, or other devices, making it almost impossible to track them down.

Shortly thereafter, a "Missing Women List" was started, which included all of Vancouver, and the number of women on it grew so fast that the task force doubled in size in a month, then doubled again in two more months. The list was narrowed down specifically for the Low Track area. A total of sixteen women had been reported missing at that time. But, the number would mushroom just three years later (2001) to fifty-four women on the list. 2001 was significant because it marked the year the first arrest was made in the case (We will look into this more later). Sadly, it became very clear that, at a minimum, the police were looking for a sexual predator, likely male, and someone who frequented the Low Track area. Detective Dickson's investigative mind also recalled that none of the women or their bodies had been seen, in most cases, for years. Dickson would later state that he was certain the majority, if not all of the women on the Missing Women List were dead and speculated that they were likely murdered.

Local, and sometimes international media took a hold of the story about the sharp increase of missing women and ran pieces periodically. They'd pointed out that law enforcement was worried about the lifestyle women were living in Vancouver's Downtown Eastside, and that the number of women being reported as missing from the area had tripled in three years.

Even with the press coverage, investigators had a difficult time trying to build a case because female victims of sexual or physical assault were too scared to cooperate, and the pimps or drug pushers refused to talk to the police. Prostitutes would be found in dumpsters, beaten and left for dead, and still they would not talk. Some speculated that the person doing these heinous acts might know something about the missing women. But, as soon as these women were able to function, they'd be seen back on the streets looking for work or drugs. In addition, they were not interested in helping the police find the people responsible for the crimes against them or their friends.

Although no one wanted to admit it, and the majority of the cases were classified as "missing persons" cases, the members of the task force grew more confident each day that these women were being systematically hunted. Because of this, they felt they were now trying to put a face to a suspected serial killer. It was suggested that surveillance teams be assembled and work the area to see if they could figure out what was happening. Some of the surveillance lasted for twenty-four hour periods. The workload increased, forcing the task force to be staffed with more officers (over 85 investigators at one point). Unbelievably, not a single strong lead was developed despite the surveillance, or the press coverage, or the increase in manpower. In fact, during this same time period, more and more women were disappearing, usually without a trace. Two things became crystal clear: law enforcement was in way over their heads, and they were no closer to identifying the perpetrator.

The case stretched over two decades, during periods in American history involving serial killers near the Canadian border; task force investigators tried another route to solve this case. They began focusing on other sexual predators and serial killers that may have visited Canada or been relatively close by. They hoped to get a break or establish similar patterns in other cases that they were seeing in their case. If they were lucky, it might lead them to a suspect.

Among the individuals considered as possible suspects for the Low Track Missing Persons case were Gary Leon Ridgway aka

"Green River Killer," Dayton Leroy Rogers aka "Molalla Forest Killer," Keith Hunter Jesperson aka "The Happy Face Killer," Robert Yates (convicted of killing thirteen prostitutes in nearby Seattle), and convicted rapist John Eric Armstrong. Investigators from each of these cases were contacted, but no evidence was obtained that could put any of these killers in Vancouver's Downtown Eastside.

A final suspect, Ronald Richard McCauley, a twice-convicted rapist with ties to Low Track, was also considered. He's believed to have killed four Low Track prostitutes in 1995 and 1996; however, although listed as the primary suspect on four murder cases, he has never been formally charged with murder. I'm not sure how someone is listed as the primary suspect for four murders, but is never charged. My guess is the investigators have not located their bodies or do not have enough probable cause to charge McCauley at this time.

Running out of options for their case, investigators began to look again into Robert and David Pickton. Their names came up often previously because David had a sexual assault conviction and Robert was known to frequent the Low Track area to pick up hookers. Investigators had suspicions about the brothers mostly based on hearsay and definitely not enough to act upon.

The place where the brothers called home, Piggy Palace, was known by police to host wild parties, and several prostitutes from Low Track were spotted there. But it wasn't until it was later revealed that Piggy Palace was the crime scene where David Pickton had sexually assaulted a woman that they took a stronger interest into the property and the Pickton brothers. Despite the efforts of the task force, nothing concrete linking the brothers to the disappearance of any of the Low Track women was discovered. This bothered everyone involved. Investigators knew the Picktons were up to no good but couldn't prove anything.

The investigation went stagnant and was stretching for years, making people angry as frustration boiled over. Then, like many of my cases and other large-scale cases I've worked, the task force investigators caught a huge break when a man named Bill Hiscox contacted them. He told them he thought Robert Pickton was responsible for all the missing women from Low Track, but he wasn't squeaky clean himself.

Bill Hiscox had turned to drugs and alcohol after his wife passed away and had befriended Robert and his brother because they provided him with drugs and a place to sleep. Hiscox became a party animal while trying to deal with the loss of his wife, and the Pickton brothers threw great parties, so they got along great. Investigators were leery of Hiscox, though, because he told them he was being helped off of drugs and was "sort of adopted" by an older woman who turned out to be the on-again, off-again girlfriend of Robert Pickton. Police wondered if Hiscox was scorned or if he had other motives to implicate the Picktons as being somehow involved with the missing women from Low Track.

Hiscox was persistent and convinced the police that he was coming forward based on the stories he was reading in the newspaper about disappearing women. He described Robert Pickton as a quiet guy who was difficult to talk to and "had no use for men." This statement confused the investigators, but it was clear as they listened to Hiscox that Robert was "different."

When pressed, Hiscox described Piggy Palace as a "creepy-looking place" patrolled by a ferocious 600-pound wild boar. He also told investigators that Robert was charged with attempted murder in 1997 (a fact they seemed to have missed, dismissed, or failed to consider) when it was alleged that he stabbed a prostitute (again a huge clue), Wendy Lynn Eistetter, at the pig farm. Eistetter said she was handcuffed and freed herself after stabbing Robert but that Robert had stabbed her several times. However, in January 1998, the case was dismissed because the prosecutor was concerned the victim (Eistetter) would not be a good witness. The prosecutor thought her testimony would not hold up in court based on the fact she was a heavy drug user... and a prostitute.

Investigators learned from Hiscox that Robert had purses and identification cards "of all kinds of women" in his trailer on the farm and would visit downtown Vancouver "to pick up women often." Eventually, VPD and the RCMP (who also had joined the task force in early part of 1999) gathered enough probable cause to conduct three searches at Piggy Palace. Unfortunately, the searches revealed no clues or evidence related to the numerous missing women from Low Track. Investigators felt confident that Robert Pickton was involved with the missing women, but when the searches revealed nothing, the whole investigation seemed to be crippled, like the wind had been sucked from their sails.

Regardless of the setback, Robert and his brother remained on the list of possible suspects. Oddly, however, they were not under surveillance after this, and there was an increase in the number of women being reported as missing. Investigators felt they were on the right track with the Pickton brothers, but then almost two years went by, right in the middle of the investigation, in which no new reports of missing women surfaced. Some speculated the searches at Piggy Palace may have influenced Robert Pickton to lay low, but then again, they had no proof of that and no true idea of what Robert was really up to. All they knew was he spent a lot of time at Low Track, picked up prostitutes, and brought them back to his farm to give them drugs.

Finally, in 2002, when everyone was grasping at straws and pulling their teeth out trying to crack the Low Track case, a monumental discovery was made. It changed the atmosphere of the task force, and they finally had the evidence they needed to go after Robert Pickton. What followed will forever be talked about in the true crime community and should serve as a reminder for law enforcement in Canada, and internationally, to always be diligent during investigations, even when the victims live lifestyles we find repulsive.

Illustration 3: The Farm

February 7, 2002, investigators from the task force again searched Piggy Palace, and the property line adjacent to Piggy Palace (which was owned by one of the few friends Robert Pickton had) and make a grisly discovery shaking the Vancouver community. The bodies of Sereena Abotsway and Mona Wilson were discovered. This alone was terrible, but it was the fact that their bodies had been butchered that caused the investigators to worry. These women were on the Missing Women List, so it was assumed more of the women on the list likely had met a similar fate.

The media began reporting, which was strange because the information was being guarded, that not only were two bodies found, but there were other body parts being found, and placed the blame on Robert Pickton. At the time of the search, Robert Pickton was in custody on an illegal weapons charge, but he was later released after posting bail on that case. Interestingly enough, he was placed on constant surveillance when he left the jail because investigators now believed he was somehow related to their case.

On February 22, 2002, Robert Pickton was again arrested, but this time he was charged with two counts of first degree murder (Abotsway and Wilson). It took fifteen days to arrest Robert, which caused wide-spread speculation as to why. But, having worked over one-hundred homicide cases, I know I don't seek an arrest warrant for murder unless I have an overwhelming amount of evidence, and I'm one-hundred percent sure the person who committed the murder is the person I'm seeking the arrest warrant for. I personally believe, given the amount of work put into this investigation and case, investigators did not want to foul it up this close to finally apprehending a suspect, which explains the length of time to secure the arrest warrant. I'd wait even longer if it meant I could truly nail the suspect with as strong a case as I could build.

Amazingly (and sadly), Robert Pickton's arrest for two murders was only the beginning. He'd end up being Canada's most notorious serial killer and the worst in their history to date. The case already had national attention at this point, but tension had grown over the years and boiled over after Robert Pickton was finally arrested for murder.[4] Wide-spread grief was shared by friends and family members who had relatives on the Missing Women List, and heated speculation and dissension regarding how the Vancouver Police Department and others handled the investigation clouded the discussions about how to move forward.

On April 2, 2002, as further evidence was located on the 14-acre pig farm, Robert Pickton was charged with three more murders (Jacqueline McDonell, Diane Rock and Heather Bottomley). He still hadn't been arraigned in court for the two original counts noted above, but the evidence of multiple murders was mounting, and investigators believed far more evidence would be located as they searched his property.

On April 9, 2002, the murders of Andrea Joesbury and Brenda Wolfe were added to Robert Pickton's charges. This was based on DNA evidence located at the farm.

On September 20, 2002, evidence obtained from his properties resulted in four more charges of murder against Robert

Pickton (Georgina Papin, Patricia Johnson, Helen Hallmark and Jennifer Furminger).

On October 3, 2002, a human head and hands, later positively identified as belonging to Mona Wilson, were discovered on his farm, and Robert Pickton was charged formally in court with four more murders (Heather Gabrielle Chinnock, Tanya Marlo Holyk, Sherry Irving, and Inga Monique Hall).

By the beginning of 2004, as the remains of a total of 30 women had been located on his farm, Robert Pickton was now facing 22 counts of murder and 15 counts of first degree murder (some of the remains were unidentifiable at that time explaining the discrepancy of the charges). It was later released, and confirmed through police reports, that body parts were located in a wood chipper on the property, and a jaw bone was located in a pig pen, confirming some of the early eerie speculation that Robert Pickton was butchering the victims and feeding them to his pigs. Further, if things weren't already quite bizarre, police also confirmed that human remains were located in a freezer next to unsold meat.

By October of 2004, the 21-month search of Robert Pickton's farm conducted by over

100 anthropologists linked, through DNA, a large group of women who were on the Missing Women List. In addition, an internal report was leaked speculating that some of the remains of the victims were mixed with the pig meat Pickton and his brother and sister were selling from the farm, meaning people purchasing meat from the Picktons (or neighbors getting the meat for free) may have actually consumed some of the victims.[10] At this time, six more known victims (Yvonne Boen, Dawn Crey, Wendy Crawford, Andrea Borhaven, Kerry Koski, and Cara Ellis) were identified through their remains on the property, and their murders were charged to Robert Pickton.

Around the same time, *The Toronto Star* released a report indicating a possible MO for serial killer Robert Pickton, which captivated readers because no one could figure out how or why Pickton had allegedly done what police said he did.[5] Among the details of the report, it was alleged that Robert would entice prostitutes to his farm and was generous to them because he gave them drugs, cooked for them, and threw lavish wild parties in their honor. Strangely, by all accounts, even verified through Bill Hiscox,

Robert did not drink or use drugs until around 2001. He developed a serious crack cocaine habit, which many believe contributed to why he committed such heinous crimes. He kept to himself mostly but had a great affection for the prostitutes he brought to his farm and had sex with them all. He'd seen so many of them using drugs that he began to experiment with drugs himself. Even armed with all this information, the public still didn't understand his fully deviant and unabashed behavior.

Investigators, anthropologists, and police continued to search Robert Pickton's properties almost twenty-four hours a day after the first human remains were located. It was a daunting task, but the work needed to be done, and new evidence was recovered daily.

Although many citizens were frustrated about how the case had been handled up until then, they were supportive of how the case was being handled at the time and shared less public criticism regarding the Vancouver Police Department and Royal Canadian Mounted Police. There was a small sense of relief among all the parties involved because the monster (Robert Pickton was being labelled as a monster after the first news report broke regarding the human remains discovered on his farm) was locked in custody and could not murder more women. This was a good thing because it would take months to sort out the sick and demented pieces of Robert's life, what he did, and to find what was left of the victims.

On May 26, 2005, 12 more charges were filed against Robert Pickton for the killings of Cara Ellis, Andrea Borhaven, Debra Lynne Jones, Marnie Frey, Tiffany Drew, Kerry Koski, Sarah de Vries, Cynthia Feliks, Angela Jardine, Wendy Crawford, Diana Melnick, and Jane Doe (an unidentified woman) bringing the total number of first-degree murder charges to 27. Each new charge lodged against Robert Pickton caused people to shake their heads in bewilderment because they couldn't wrap their minds around one man killing so many women. People wanted to hear more but were afraid of what they might hear.

The task of processing the crime scenes proved almost too much, as the cost for the project skyrocketed to over $70 million, and hundreds of thousands of pieces of evidence were being collected. Investigators continued to move forward, despite the long hours because they needed to identify every victim they could in order to bring closure to the friends and families, many of whom should have been thanked for being so persistent about their missing loved ones.

As the process continued, legal battles were heating up as to who would represent Robert Pickton and how many prosecutors would be assigned to the case. Various motions were filed from both sides, further clogging up the system and slowing down the judicial process. And, from day one, Robert's defense team stated publicly that their client maintained he was innocent and they would provide evidence that other people were involved in the grisly murders. Again the public began to demand action as the process was taking too long and they wanted Robert to pay for what he did.

Finally, in January of 2006, the much-anticipated trial against Robert Pickton began amidst turmoil, speculation, and outrage. He'd require law enforcement escorts at all times (people wanted him dead for what he had done). The whole court case would be a costly endeavor filled with lies, deceit, questionable evidence, and suspect witnesses. Justice James Williams had no idea how much work hearing Pickton's case would require, but it was clear that the public, and the friends and family of the victims, needed closure and were not going to rest until he was convicted. The defense estimated the trial would take six months, while the prosecution gave an original estimation of eight months. Both were off, as it would take almost a full year to hear all the evidence and witnesses in the matter. Each step of the process was featured in local and international news, and once Justice Williams lifted the media ban, all hell would break loose.

Illustration 4: The interior of a trailer parked on the Picktons' farm. The blood of Mona Wilson (victim) was found inside

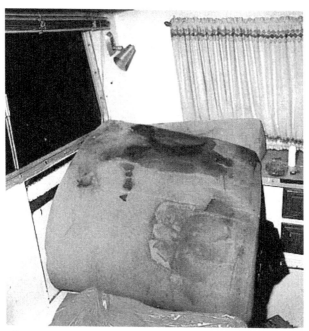

Illustration 5: Blood-stained mattress found inside trailer on the farm

Canadian Police were contacted in 1999 by a "friend of Robert's" who stated he had seen human remains in a freezer belonging to Robert. The reporting party described the remains, the freezer, and the location of the freezer on the farm. Police interviewed Pickton at Piggy Palace, and he gave them consent to search his pig farm. Apparently Robert had nothing to hide, or maybe he was tired of what he had been doing and wanted to be discovered. For an unknown reason, even up to today, the police officers did not search the farm at that time. Many of the families of the victims in this case were very upset when they learned about this and they still haven't received an explanation as to why a search wasn't conducted. Looking back on the case, it seems several murders could have been prevented had the police searched and located human remains on the property. I suspect we will never know why a search wasn't done. My thought is if Robert Pickton was the main suspect for the case, the police may have wanted to gather more evidence prior to searching the farm and alerting Robert that he was under investigation.

In 2003, a second Preliminary Inquiry was held regarding Robert Pickton. The contents of the hearing were covered by a publication ban until 2010. Essentially, it was revealed that Pickton was charged with attempted murder after an altercation with a prostitute in 1997 at Piggy Palace. The woman said she was driven to Pickton's pig farm by Robert, they had sex, and afterwards, he placed handcuffs on one of her hands and handcuffed her to the bed. He then stabbed her in the abdomen several times. She said she was able to get a hold of a knife and stab Robert in self-defense, and when he stopped, she was able to free herself.

The report said she ran from the farm and was picked up by an unknown person who gave her a ride to the local hospital. Shortly thereafter, Robert showed up at the same hospital to be treated for his wounds. The key for the handcuff on her wrist was located in Robert Pickton's pants pocket.

This charge was stayed, however, because the woman had drug addiction issues and the prosecutor didn't believe he could get a conviction with her courtroom testimony. If the prosecution can't put on a case they believe they can win, they normally won't try it. Although the charge was stayed, clothes and rubber boots Robert wore the night of the attack were collected as evidence and stored for seven years. After he was arrested, investigators retrieved this evidence and swabbed it for DNA. The results indicated that DNA on the boots worn by Robert Pickton during this event matched two women who were on the Missing Women List (specifically from the Low Track area).

So, during the prelimary hearing on January 30, 2006, Pickton was facing 27 counts of first-degree murder. Through his attorneys, he immediately pled not guilty to all 27 charges of first-degree murder and claimed the Crown had arrested the wrong person.

At night, he sat smugly in a jail cell claiming innocence while his popularity skyrocketed. Letters of "fans" and people disgusted by him flooded the facility. He was placed in protective custody to protect him against inmates who also found him repulsive.

The voir dire for the trial was expected to last almost a year; however, on March 2,

Justice James Williams rejected one of the first-degree murder counts due to the lack of evidence. In addition, on August 9, Justice Williams split the remaining twenty-six charges into two groups. One group contained six counts of first-degree murder, and the other group included the remaining 20 counts of first-degree murder.[6] Justice Williams explained that each count could be heard separately, but he had the ability to change things and was doing so. So, concerned about the cost of the trial, the fact a trial would be such a large burden on the jurors (he estimated it would take over two years for such a trial), and during such time, a mistrial was a greater possibility, he split the cases into two. Justice Williams noted the evidence for the six counts were "materially different" than the other 20 counts anyway.[7]

Therefore, the case against Robert Pickton regarding six counts of first-degree murder would be heard in Justice Williams's court room. He would later say the trial was fun for him, although he noted it was quite complex and he was not impressed by the antics carried on by the defense and the prosecution. The proceedings just to get to the actual trial date took over a year to be heard and ruled upon. During that time, Robert Pickton became even more popular among serial killer groupies and the equally demented people within our society. It was a full-time job managing inmate Pickton. The jail staff and deputies assigned to the case would quickly grow tired of Robert, his demands, and the amount of work he created for them.

On January 22, 2007, Robert Pickton sat in court staring at six counts of first-degree murder for victims Frey, Abotsway, Papin, Joesbury, Wolfe, and Wilson. This was a significant day in the case because up until this point, there was a media ban for all proceedings regarding defendant Robert Pickton. This means all the stories coming out for the last year and a half were based completely on speculation. After some of the discovery was revealed in court, which included several of the first gory details of this brutal case, the media began salivating because they'd finally be able to discuss this case openly. Within hours, details were released to the public and immediately people following the case who thought they had seen and heard everything, had their jaws drop.

26 WOMEN, ONE MAN CHARGED IN THEIR DEATHS

Illustration 6: Victims of Pickton

Even to the most hardened investigator, the details of what Robert was alleged to have done were unbearable: human skulls sawed in half, filled with hands and feet from other human victims; human remains found stuffed into a garbage bag while blood-laden clothing was found in Pickton's personal trailer; part of a victim's jawbone and teeth found in a pig pen near Pickton's slaughterhouse; and a .22 caliber handgun with a dildo attached to the muzzle containing both his and a victim's DNA. Pickton later stated during a recorded statement that he attached the dildo to the weapon to act as a silencer.[8] Details like these made it clear that Robert Pickton was a monster, but as the case wore on, his attorneys did their best to implicate several of his associates as the murderer, not him.

By February 2007, significant pieces of evidence had been admitted at the trial, which included items police found inside Pickton's trailer during the last search warrant they executed: a loaded .22 revolver with a dildo over the barrel and one round fired, "Spanish Fly" aphrodisiac; boxes of .357 Magnum handgun ammunition; night-vision googles; two pairs of faux fur-lined handcuffs; and a syringe with three milliliters of a blue liquid (investigators suspected the fluid was windshield wiper fluid). Lab staff testified that about 80 unidentified DNA profiles, roughly half male and half female, were discovered on evidence from the crime scene; photographs showing remains of Mona Wilson in a garbage can found in the suspect's slaughterhouse; a videotaped interview of Pickton's friend, witness Scott Chubb (more details on this witness to follow below) telling police that Pickton told him a good way to kill a female heroin addict was to inject her with windshield washer fluid; and a second tape in which an associate of Pickton's, Andrew Bellwood, said Pickton mentioned killing prostitutes by handcuffing and strangling them, then bleeding and gutting them before feeding them to pigs.

The more the case was presented, the more everyone involved wished it would end. Experts on both sides were brought in to testify, and at times, the jurors were slammed with so much information, and unfathomable facts that the judge had to give them recesses to let them rest before plodding on. At one point, the jurors were given a two-week vacation because it was clear they were fatigued and needed time to process everything they'd heard or seen up to that point.

On May 10, after 78 witnesses had taken the stand, the people on the jury learned that one of the victims, Brenda Wolfe, the mother of two, had asked for government assistance for food because she'd spent what little money she had to make a good Christmas for her kids. This was a move by the prosecution to demonstrate the victims were good-hearted people too. It made the victims more real, and provided the jurors faces and souls to go with the body parts found on Robert Pickton's farm. It was mentioned several times in court that, although the victims were prostitutes, they also had lives and families and were people nonetheless.

The prosecution team made it clear that they were going to continue to get the victims the attention they deserved and brought in Elaine Allen to testify. Allen, employed at Women's Information Safe House (WISH) drop-in center knew five of the victims. She told the jury how Andrea spoke softly and Georgina Papin was charming and outspoken; how the opinionated Sereena often showed signs of physical abuse and had numerous tracks from drug use, and Mona had a boyfriend who sent her out to make money. Andrea had been the best-behaved client she'd ever had, being both polite and aware of the needs of others. Allen and Andrea spent a lot of their time talking about Andrea's difficult life. Obviously Allen made friendships with the victims, and providing her testimony was challenging and emotional.

Once the foundation was set that the victims were good people despite having to turn to prostitution to pay bills or support drug habits, the prosecution team switched gears and offered an overwhelming amount of evidence as to what they believed Robert Pickton had done with the bodies of the women he'd killed.

Jim Cress, a driver for a Vancouver rendering company, was brought in to testify about his dealing with Robert Pickton. He explained that he had picked up two or five (he couldn't recall the number) 45-gallon barrels of pork offal and burnt meat chunks from the Pickton farm and took them to West Coast Reduction. Cress explained that before 2002, customers could dump stuff at the plant themselves, unsupervised, and he'd seen Pickton there once. The prosecution offered that Robert was disposing of pieces of the victims he'd murdered at the plant. While Cress's testimony was suggestive, the defense hammered it. The defense pointed out that Robert and his family owned a pig farm, where they butchered animals and sold the meat. Many farmers doing the same thing in the area used the services of Mr. Cress and visited West Coast Reduction. It was clear the witness's statement wasn't damaging as substantive evidence; however, the image of bodies being placed in barrels and shipped off to be destroyed seemed plausible and likely stayed with the jurors.

The battle between the defense and prosecution was intense. Justice Williams continually handled objections from both sides, and had to warn the teams to remain professional. Both sides would let comments slip that shouldn't have, forcing the Justice to instruct the jury to forget what they just heard. The media speculated the defense was doing a great job of squashing the prosecution team's witnesses. Hoping to bolster their case, the prosecution team brought in two of their "star" witnesses, Pat Casanova and Scott Chubb.

Pat Casanova migrated to Canada from the Philippines and quickly became well known in the Vancouver underworld for selling pig meat and arranging cock fights. He got the pig meat from Robert Pickton or butchered it himself on Robert's farm, and the cock fights occurred on Robert's property. The prosecution knew Casanova was a close associate of Robert's, and although they knew he would be heavily scrutinized during cross-examination, they felt it was worth the risk to introduce him. Casanova explained to the prosecution team that he had damaging information pertaining to what Robert was doing at Piggy Palace that he obtained while being at the farm numerous times.

Strangely enough, but not uncommon during criminal proceedings and investigations as large as this case, Casanova was actually arrested during the Missing Women case. Investigators had connected him to fifteen of the women on the Missing Women List. However, he was later released and never charged with any crimes. Now he was in court testifying against his friend. It's not uncommon for law enforcement to arrest someone related to a case, then later offer them some sort of deal or persuade them to testify against another person in the same case. Sometimes these people have their own charges dropped or lowered, or even receive financial compensation for such a deal. It's a dirty part of law enforcement, one the public has no knowledge of, and continues to be used during investigations and court proceedings. I've done this in my career. I justify it by setting an end point in a case. If I was looking to obtain a murder conviction, and the majority of my evidence was circumstantial, I would do everything I could, within legal guidelines, to obtain evidence or testimony to secure the conviction.

Casanova would testify that he saw Robert Pickton use the exact freezer in which the investigators had located female body parts next to butchered pig meat. He said he saw Robert use the freezer on at least one occasion. However, on cross examination, Casanova admitted that he butchered pigs for several years (and knew the Picktons for two decades) at Piggy Palace. He also said he likely used the same freezer the body parts had been found in. The light switch flipped in Casanova's head and he spontaneously declared he never saw any human body parts, in any freezer, on the property.

The defense team began to steamroll Casanova. Casanova originally said he knew nothing about Robert's sexual activities on the farm and had never been in his trailer. He also stated that he (Casanova) never had contact with prostitutes and he never engaged in sexual activity with the prostitutes. It later came out in court, after aggressive cross-examination, that Casanova actually had paid for oral sex with at least four of the same women Robert Pickton was being charged with their murders.

Originally the prosecution team had thought they were done with Casanova's testimony, but after the defense had damaged his credibility, the prosecution asked to question him again.

The prosecution turned to discussing the various articles of women's clothing located by the investigators. Casanova said he'd noticed items of clothing in the trailer, including some purses that he believed belonged to women who were not present. Then he offered that Pickton had never spoken with him about missing women, so he wasn't sure who the property belonged to.

Casanova also stated that he'd known Robert Pickton for approximately two decades and had only seen him angry one time. It seemed as though Casanova was trying to help Robert instead of send him away for murder. And, while the prosecution team was trying to rebuild Casanova's character, he'd just made conflicting statements and the defense team had noticed.

The defense team was allowed to cross-examine Casanova again. Their intent was to totally destroy Casanova's character and, with a little luck, convince the jury that he (Casanova) was actually a likely suspect for the murder of Dinah Taylor (aka "Angel). Once it was clear that Mr. Casanova was not truthful, he became an easy target.

When first asked by police, Casanova said he had sex with one woman named "Roxanne" while at Piggy Palace, but he later said it was four women. He did not mention Dinah Taylor, aka Angel, but it appeared he may have been the last person to see her alive. Based on this, the jury was able to determine that Casanova would lie to protect himself at all costs. He was deemed an un-credible witness because he had told an officer he never lied, but it was demonstrated time and again, under oath, that he lied. His response when asked about not being truthful was that he was "forgetful at times."

Working toward creating doubt in the minds of the jury, the defense continued to try to connect Casanova to some of the suspected murders. He was asked why his DNA was located on a slaughterhouse door. He said it was from his mucous as it spewed out after his throat treatments for cancer. He was asked if he used orange bags to carry out butchered pigs. He denied using them. The defense was trying to tie Casanova into the orange bags because a victim's DNA was found on similar bags on the farm.

Eventually, the defense team was told by Justice Williams that witness Casanova was not charged with murder and was not on trial for murder, and therefore, they needed to stop trying to question him as though he was. Consequently, the defense team backed down, but it was painfully clear to the jury that Casanova's testimony was deeply flawed and full of lies.

During Casanova's testimony, and while he was seated in the courtroom during the trial, Robert and Casanova would make casual eye contact with each other and were seen smiling at one another. To this day, according to Robert, he considers Casanova a friend and has no ill will toward the man for testifying against him. It's my opinion, based on what Casanova originally stated to the police and prosecutor with regard to Mr. Pickton, and what he later said in court, that Casanova intended to confuse the jury. Although the defense clearly established Casanova was a liar, enough circumstantial evidence from his testimony had to make at least a few of the jurors cringe knowing there was far more than pig butchering going on at Piggy Palace.

The prosecution team was reeling and needed a boost in court. They pushed forward with their next star witness, Scott Chubb, in an effort to get the multiple murder case against Robert Pickton back on track.

Scott Chubb had spent a considerable amount of time at the pig farm and later became an employee of Robert Pickton. He told the police that they could record his statement and that Robert had made several dark comments that led him to believe Robert was involved with the missing women from Low Track. The testimony was moving along fairly well, but the defense objected to a certain line of questioning and the Justice asked why.

The defense team offered that Chubb was a paid informant and was providing his testimony purely for money.

A hush was heard in the courtroom. The prosecution team offered that Chubb had been a paid informant, but it was for a different case.

The defense countered that the case was different but involved Robert Pickton. The prosecution asked to approach the Justice. After a brief discussion, the defense's objection was over ruled and the testimony continued.

I've used numerous informants in my career. My main goal is to protect their identity. However, when it comes to a murder case, especially like the one against Robert Pickton, it is likely the identity of a confidential informant is only revealed based on the magnitude of the case. In this case, information from Chubb was used to secure a search warrant allowing officers to search Robert's property for a forbidden firearm and was not related to the case being heard.

Constable Nathan Wells cultivated Chubb as an informant, paying him $1,450 altogether, and used his information (some of which would turn out to be false) on several cases unrelated to Robert Pickton. Wells said that, at the time, he was unaware that Robert Pickton was a suspect in the disappearance of women from Eastside Vancouver. He believed only that he was confiscating a forbidden gun.

Prosecutor Geoff Baragar tried to paint a picture with Chubb, an admitted ex-heroin junkie, in an effort to show that he and Robert were friends and they had several interesting conversations. Chubb said Pickton told him a woman named Lynn Ellingsen was costing him a lot of money and he wanted Chubb to "talk" to her. Chubb took the statement to mean Robert wanted him to stop her, at any cost and by any means, from continuing to cost him money. Chubb said he was hesitant and Robert offered him $1000 to take care of this favor for him, but that was only the beginning of the disturbing talks between Chubb and Pickton.

As they continued to talk, Chubb said Robert told him that it was easy to kill drug addicts because they already had tracks and needle marks. Robert continued to say if a person injected windshield washer fluid in these women, they'd die and the police would probably dismiss their death as an overdose. This statement was damaging because the jury had already learned that a syringe containing windshield wiper fluid was located in Robert's trailer.

Once the prosecutor was done, things again turned south for this witness. While being cross-examined, one of Robert's attorneys, Peter Richie, put Chubb on the spot. His mission was to show that Chubb would say whatever the prosecution wanted him to say and was doing so to get paid. A series of objections were included in this cross-examination. Richie continued to ask Chubb if he was being paid for his testimony or if he was trying to get paid for his testimony. Chubb said he was trying to get money, but he was doing so to secure protection for him and his family because Robert's brother, David, threatened him and had come after him once already. Chubb denied being paid as an informant, but the defense entered police records indicating he was paid specifically for information. As Richie continued to poke holes in Chubb's statement, Chubb stated he suffered a serious head injury and the injury was likely what caused the discrepancies.

When asked if he knew anything about guns, Chubb said no and that he only handled Robert Pickton's gun one time. However, Chubb had a conviction for possession of an unregistered firearm on his rap sheet. He told police he had witnessed a forbidden weapon on Robert's farm, a Mac-10 to be exact. His information was used to secure a search warrant for Robert's trailer at Piggy Palace. He then said Constable Wells was confused about what he said (referring to the forbidden weapon) and that he had only heard of the weapon and not actually seen it with Robert or at his farm.

When asked why he even went to the police about Robert Pickton, especially since they were such close friends, Chubb stated he was hopeful the police would go after a drug dealer (Robert Pickton) to help get his girlfriend off cocaine. It was becoming clear that Chubb's statements were inconsistent and all over the place. The discrepancies in what Chubb was stating caused confusion for the jury, which damaged the prosecution's case.

Unlike the bond between Casanova and Robert, the relationship was clearly different between Robert and Chubb. Robert, who normally didn't show much emotion, nor did much while almost one hundred witnesses gave their testimony in his trial, paid close attention to Chubb. As the defense team grilled Chubb, Robert was seen cracking a tiny smile as Chubb struggled and looked silly in court. There was serious tension between Chubb and Robert. I was unable to unearth what their beef was about, but it was certainly real. At one point, while Chubb was being embarrassed by the defense team, Chubb was seen glaring at Robert and spontaneously declared, "Go ahead and attack my character; I'm not the one on trial for six counts of murder."

Again, the prosecution's case took a hit. It was obvious the star witnesses they had presented (Casanova and Chubb) were not as stellar as Prosecutor Baragar had hoped. Instead of providing clear and concise statements and demonstrating strong evidence for the jury to consider that Robert was a murderer, confusion and speculation plagued the case. Baragar needed help and turned to his final witness, Andrew Bellwood, hoping he'd be able to make sense of this bizarre case and convince the jury the defendant was guilty of murder.

Andrew Bellwood was the 97th witness in the Robert Pickton first-degree murder trial. His testimony was a milestone for many reasons. First, his testimony would be attacked by Robert's attorney and unlike Casanova and Chubb, it would hold up; and secondly, the papers reported the case had cost the Crown over $100 million, which marked it the most expensive case in Canadian history.

When being questioned, Bellwood was described as being very matter-of-fact, cavalier even, as he described how he had dinner with Pickton in 1999. He said the day after the dinner, they met up again and Robert described how he had killed prostitutes then fed their remains to his pigs. Bellwood said Robert had sex with them, and murdered them on the farm. He said Robert would hack off their body parts and toss them to the pigs. He said other body parts were mixed in barrels with pig entrails and later dumped at a disposal plant. Bellwood said Robert explained the process so naturally that it was clear he'd been doing it for a long time. When prosecutor Barager asked Bellwood to explain what he meant, Bellwood said Robert lured them to the farm with the drug of their choice, had sex with them, killed them, and disposed of their bodies or fed them to the pigs. Bellwood's testimony was convincing and well-delivered.

Unlike Chubb and Casanova, Bellwood was able to shed light on what Robert did to his victims. He said Robert would gag his victims and use handcuffs or wire with looped ends to secure them to his bed in his trailer. Bellwood stated, "He (Robert) would put the victims into the doggy-style position, have intercourse with them, then kill them…" for no apparent reason. The manner in which Bellwood relayed the story was convincing, and he added that, "As he (Robert) was telling me the story, it was almost like there was a woman on the bed. It was like a play. Robert was reliving the experience and it was clear he'd done what he said he did to those women."

Feeling good about his case, the prosecutor turned his witness over to the defense for cross-examination. Defense attorney Adrian Brooks explained to the jurors that he found it hard to believe Pickton would describe such disgusting events to Mr. Bellwood, but then right after allegedly sharing such a disturbing story, Mr. Bellwood stayed and ate a meal with him. Brooks pointed out that they allegedly ate pork and wondered why Mr. Bellwood would allegedly eat pork with Robert after he supposedly told him he killed these women and fed their bodies to the pigs.

Bellwood did not waiver and stated Robert was a "nice fellow" who loaned him money and he thought originally that Robert had fabricated the story about murdering and butchering the prostitutes. He said he didn't go to the police right away because he (Bellwood) was using drugs at the time, and he didn't want to get himself in trouble.

Defense attorney Brooks didn't stop there. He noted that Bellwood previously said he was alone with Robert during the dark discussion they had, but during another part of the same testimony he (Bellwood) said Lynn Ellingsen was with them. Bellwood countered with stating that he would not have gone through all that he had gone through over the last five years (referring to numerous interviews with police and the prosecution team) to get into court to lie about it, and he offered that he had simply confused two events. His position was that Ellingsen was likely present for something else and was not present during the conversation he had with Robert when he talked about killing prostitutes.

Lastly, the defense team pointed out that Bellwood was heavily addicted to crack cocaine at the time he allegedly heard the story about the victims and that it was likely he was in an impaired state and confused what Robert had told him. Bellwood admitted to using crack cocaine but said it did not affect what he remembered Robert telling him. In addition, Bellwood noted that he didn't have much money and no real place to live, but he moved out shortly after Robert's admission because his comments caused him great concern.

The prosecution had successfully re-built their case against Robert Pickton, and they had a key piece of evidence, by the way of testimony, that they presented next.

An undercover agent, posing as a criminal, was booked into the facility where Robert Pickton was being held. The agent was able to have a conversation with Robert in the holding area of the facility. The conversation took place as Robert's case was being heard. The undercover agent explained that Robert Pickton admitted to him that he killed 49 female prostitutes. This was damaging for Robert's case, but there was more. The undercover agent said Robert told him his only regret was that he didn't kill 50 women. The agent asked him why that was. Robert said he idolized serial killer, Gary Ridgway, and he wanted to have, "one more than Gary." Robert also told the agent that the only reason he'd been caught was because he'd gotten "sloppy." Obviously this testimony blew the jury away.

The defense tried to attack the statement by stating Robert was not aware of what he was saying and may have said what he said trying to outwardly appear like he was some sort of star based on his case being so high-profile. The defense also said Robert was not intelligent and therefore, could not make such a statement. The defense's efforts with regard to this testimony fell on deaf ears. Robert appeared to have nailed his own coffin while blabbing to the undercover agent.

Lastly, closing arguments were heard, and the judge gave the jury their instructions which he read from a large binder containing hundreds of pages of instructions. Both sides had presented so much evidence, and there were so many testimonies, that the judge had to work diligently to ensure the jury instructions were clear, concise, and that each juror understood them.

It surprised many, though, how long the jury deliberated in the Robert Pickton murder case. However, it was the longest case in Canadian history, and there were 235,000 items seized, 40,000 photos taken of the crime scenes, some 600,000 exhibits from the lab, ninety-eight witnesses for the prosecution and thirty witnesses for the defense. Nearly half a million pages of documents were created, which included the backgrounds of the six victims: Mona Wilson, Brenda Wolfe, Sereena Abotsway, Andrea Joesbury, Georgina Papin, and Marnie Frey and Pickton's taped interrogation spanned over twenty hours.

During the first three days of deliberation, the jury did not ask any questions. The media and both the defense and prosecution were unsure what that meant. The media felt perhaps the jury was struggling with a legal concept or piece (or pieces) of evidence.

Then on the fourth day, Justice Williams admitted that he made an error when relaying the jury instructions and decided to re-read them to the jurors...even against the defense team's protest. This error involved an instruction he gave to the jurors when they sent him a question. The question was, "Are we able to say 'yes' [i.e., find Pickton guilty] if we infer the accused acted indirectly?" Justice Williams originally advised the jurors that they could not just say yes based on their inference that the accused acted indirectly. Justice Williams later advised the jurors that they could in fact find the accused guilty based on the question they proposed. The defense would later bring this issue up in the appeals process, but another court would support Justice William's decision. It's not uncommon for Justices/Judges to make a mistake during a case, particularly one of such magnitude.

Finally, after more than nine days of deliberations, the jury reached a verdict: Robert Pickton was found guilty on six counts of second-degree murder, but not guilty on six counts of first-degree murder. Those in the courtroom were stunned, and the families and friends of the victims were disappointed and clearly upset; the terrible saga they endured, years of court, the gruesome details, and the sheer magnitude of the case had worn them down. And, after all they'd been through, they were even more disappointed because they believed the jury, by finding Pickton guilty of second-degree murder, failed to make him answer for the victims. The verdict seemed to indicate the jury either did not believe Robert Pickton had planned out the murders or that he acted alone...but they clearly believed he was involved in at least six murders. They left the decision with regard to sentencing up to the judge. It was later learned that the jury could not agree on a first-degree conviction without an obvious smoking gun.

In Canada, a second-degree murder conviction carries a punishment of a life sentence, with no possibility of parole for a period between 10 to 25 years, which is set by the trial judge. On December 11, 2007, after reading 18 victim impact statements, British Columbia Supreme Court Judge James Williams sentenced Robert Pickton to life with no possibility of parole for 25 years —the maximum punishment for second-degree murder. This sentence is equal to the maximum sentence which could have been imposed for a first-degree murder conviction, which set some of the families and friends of the victims at ease regarding the fact the jury found him guilty only of second-degree murder. Justice Williams said during the sentencing, "Mr. Pickton's conduct was murderous and repeatedly so. I cannot know the details, but I know this: What happened to them was senseless and despicable."[9]

Unlike the murder cases I've investigated, and the majority of the ones I've read about or been given debriefs on, Robert Pickton's case is unique because a motive for the gruesome serial killings was never discovered, or even theorized, during his circus trial. Almost always a serial killer will "tell all" at some point, whether to earn credentials in the prison system, make money, become more famous, or just to fulfill sick ideations in their own minds. In this case, further speculation surfaced as to his motives, again giving the families and friends of the victims greater angst instead of closure. Everyone wanted and for that matter, needed to know why Robert did what he did.

In 2007, letters from Robert Pinkton (letters were from 2006) surfaced from a pen pal he'd made while in prison. The pen pal, Thomas Loudamy, stated he had a "hobby" of collecting correspondence with serial killers and oftentimes would pose as a fictitious person that he believed the killer would find interesting in an effort to get them to reply to him. Oddly enough, Loudamy resides in the town I do.

Loudamy, who estimated in 2006 that he had at least 300 letters from about 150 inmates, said Pickton's letters were similar to others he's received from convicted serial killers as they appear to suggest using religion to justify their actions.

Loudamy sent the letters to *The Sun*, who published pieces of them for the public to see but did not publish anything that could be deemed incriminating because Pickton was in trial at the time they published the excerpts. Here are a few (**the spelling errors are from Robert Pickton**):

"I know I was brought into this world to be hear today to change this world of there evil ways. They even want to dis-re-guard the ten command-ments from the time that Moses in his day brought in power which still is in existence today," wrote Pickton.

The second letter, written Aug. 22, 2006, again includes numerous biblical references and his interpretation of Ephesians 5:5.

"You can be sure that no immoral, impure or greedy person will in-herit the kingdom of

God .... Don't be fooled by whose who try to excuse these sins, for the terrible anger of God comes upon all those who disobey him," he said.

Ephesians 5:5 in The Jerusalem Bible reads: "For you can be quite certain that nobody who actually indulges in fornication or impurity or promiscuity — which is worshiping a false god — can inherit anything of the kingdom of God."

Some of the prostitutes who had sex with Robert Pickton testified at the trial that Robert would bring them to the farm, let them sleep in his bed without demanding sex, and would still pay them.

In addition, Crown witness Lynn Ellingsen testified she saw Robert butchering a sex-trade worker, but her credibility was destroyed during the trial.

In the religious portions, Robert refers to himself as a "condemned man of no wrong doing" just like his "father." Pickton also referred to Acts 14:22, which he interpreted as: "In each city they helped Christians to be strong and true to the faith. They told them that we must suffer many hard things to get into the holy nation of God."

Pickton told his pen-pal that he was a "fall guy," and that police arrested the wrong man:

"They are only interested in to charge any-one to get the heat off of their back and not for the truth at all," he wrote. "The police got so much money invested in this case, there will be many, many lies through-out as many things all come to surface. The police have paid many for them what to say when they are on the stand."

"But I am not worried for everything on Earth will be judged including angles. I myself is not from this world, but I am born into this world through my earthly mother and if I had to change anything I would not, for I have done no wrong," he wrote.

Pickton also brought Justice James Williams into his letters:

"They had to, they have no choice but to, if not there will be a whole lot of coart time waisted all for nothing in which there will be in need a whole lot of answers to many questions by the police and the R.C.M.P. when this coart case is over by the way of the public of when they find out that I am not in-volved at all," he wrote. "If the coart did not drop all these charges I could be in coart for at least two or more years and it really will be hard to keep a jury to-gether for so long... It could end in a mis-trial half way through coart."

However, Pickton bragged about how important he had become, referring to millions spent on his case, stating how many police and lawyers were involved, and all the evidence submitted in the case. He also pointed out that he had a large number of sheriffs who escorted him to court and provided him security when he was there. He was also provided special care while in custody.

"When I go to coart, there are three vehicles; 'my own convoy of protective excort' one vehicle is in front and one vehicle behind me of which I am in the middle vehicle. There are two sheriffs in each vehicle," he wrote. "And when I reach the coart house, there are a-nother four more sheriffs at the gates of the coart house also for my protection."

Interestingly, the letters are written as if the author is an old friend of Mya's (Loudamy's fake identity) and tenderly wishes her well. Loudamy, who maintains he has no sympathy for Pickton, said he hoped by releasing the letters publicly they'd provide a window for the public to learn more about serial killer Robert Pickton. However, law enforcement, Robert Pickton himself, and none of his representatives have verified the authenticity of the letters. *The Sun* did take the following actions attempting to confirm their authenticity:

- The outgoing stamps are consistent with those of the North Fraser Pretrial Centre(NFPC), where Pickton was being held;
- A representative of Canada Post confirmed the outgoing stamps are not forgeries; and
- The machine (identifiable with a serial number included in the stamp) used to stamp the envelopes is the machine used by the NFPC.

I had been willing to write off Robert's disturbing and unimaginable acts due to his bizarre and brutal childhood. Anyone who chooses to hide in the carcass of a hog to avoid being beaten by a parent, smells of death and decay, refuses to maintain his hygiene, and has very few social skills or friends seems to me, at least, to be a prime candidate to become a serial killer. Many known serial killers were raised in similar environments (less the fact Robert was raised on a pig farm). Robert was raised by a violent mother who in my opinion, murdered a 14-year-old child without losing a step, had a father who was only in the picture when it came time to beat Robert, and his younger brother was as dirty as him. Robert and his siblings came into money by selling a piece of Piggy Palace property, and things became considerably worse because they could now afford all the things they dreamed about but couldn't have when their parents were alive.

Although a motive for the twenty-six confirmed murders (23 believed and stated as true by Robert to an undercover agent) of Low Track prostitutes was never established in court proceedings, it's pretty obvious that at some point Robert Pickton believed he was the hand of God and, later, God himself. His statements in the letters he wrote to Loudamy clearly depict a deranged man who felt he was doing the Lord's work by murdering, butchering, and feeding the victim's to his pigs...without giving it a second thought. This went on for years, right under the noses of law enforcement. It's a tragedy all the way around.

I believe, based on all that I've read and researched, that the few "friends" Robert had, especially Pat Casanova, were equally cruel to women and likely killed some of the victims either on their own or with Robert. The atmosphere and description of Piggy Palace is something Stephen King could appreciate. Yes, it's that creepy. I also believe we will never know what truly happened at Piggy Palace, and there are likely more victims that will never be identified and put to rest in an acceptable manner while bringing closure to loved ones.

Canadian law is quite different than American law. In Canada, you can kill one or one thousand people, and the maximum time a suspect can be sentenced to is life without the possibility of parole for 25 years. At that point, you can be paroled. I firmly believe this punishment doesn't fit the crime, but I'm from the United States, and I'm a cop, so I see things differently. Canadian sentencing guidelines do not appear to successfully deter criminals from doing the nasty, terrible things they do. However, an argument over the Crown's politics and judicial structure and system seems like a concept for another book, for a different time, and likely should be argued by a Canadian, not an American. In the United States, serial killers can be sentenced to death (depending on which state tried the case and the severity of the case) or to such long sentences that the suspect can never get out. Yes, this becomes a costly burden on the state footing the bill for the suspect, but at least the suspect will never get out and have another opportunity to kill.

The manner in which Robert Pickton lured his victims to Piggy Palace by offering them drugs, to me, clearly demonstrated that he planned to murder these women and therefore, no doubt committed multiple first-degree murders. The fact he had sex with them, and then plunged a syringe full of windshield washer fluid in them to watch them die a terrible death, is deplorable and also shows intent in my mind. But it's what I believe Robert did with the victims after they were dead that places him among the very worst of criminals.

Butchering pigs is one thing, butchering humans is quite another. But Robert didn't stop there. He fed pieces of the victims to his pigs like it was no big deal, or store bodies he'd mutilated next to frozen pig meat. There are stories (difficult to confirm, though) that he served pork containing parts of his victims to customers, neighbors, and some women who later would be victims.

Although many people who followed this case wanted to believe Robert was not smart (his IQ was tested at 81), I don't buy it. I think he knew that what he was doing to the women of Low Track was completely wrong. I think he had two perversions, sex and killing. I believe he had to have sex with the victims to fulfill one perversion and would later kill them to fulfill the other. He would handcuff them with handcuffs or wire so they couldn't escape, stab them, shoot them, and stick them with syringes full of windshield washing fluid, causing them death.

There's no doubt in my mind that other people, most likely Robert's brother and some of the witnesses in this case, killed women at Piggy Palace too. I'm not sure, based on what I know of this case, why no one else was charged with murder(s) in this case. I suspect the case became too much for the Crown, the Vancouver Police Department, the Royal Canadian Mounted Patrol, and everyone else involved. Everyone had tunnel vision on Robert Pickton. Someone needed to be accountable for the murders. But, when you read everything available for this case, it's obvious other people knew exactly what happened at Piggy Palace and likely participated in the brutality and helped Robert dispose of the bodies. I can't imagine what the atmosphere was like at Piggy Palace. The women who fell for Robert's drugs and money must have been extremely desperate to even consider going there with him.

Many who have followed this case assumed Robert's brother, David, had just as much to do with women being killed at Piggy Palace as Robert did. Although he's never been charged with murder, David was recently served a civil law suit (January 2014) by nine families of the victims identified at Piggy Palace. The allegations are that he (David) knew about the killings, attempted to cover them up, and lied to police several times during their investigation. This case will undoubtedly take quite a while to be heard and adjudicated in court. It will be interesting to see how it plays out, but my guy tells me a financial settlement will be arranged and the lawsuit will be dropped.

In May of 2013, a separate lawsuit, which included thirteen families associated to convicted serial killer Robert Pickton, was brought against the Vancouver Police Department. The families alleged the Crown and VPD failed to warn women on the Downtown Eastside that a serial killer may have been on the loose. In addition, the families had numerous concerns about the manner in which VPD shared with them that their missing loved ones were linked to Robert Pickton. In March of 2014, eleven of the families settled their lawsuits with VPS for $50,000.00. This is unprecedented because somehow VPD was able to figure a murdered prostitute's life is worth $50,000.00. Two families continue to have their lawsuit against VPD at this time.

To this day, the eastside of Vancouver, aka "Low Track," is still deplorable. Women addicted to drugs still walk the streets looking to make a quick score, either sex or drugs. Drug lords still cling to blocks for their distribution, and pimps still smack these women around when they talk back or don't bring back enough money. And, no one talks to the police. A small area, geographically speaking, has been a huge problem for law enforcement for over forty years...and no end appears in sight. It's strange to even say, but oddly, the fact that Robert Pickton is in custody does not make Low Track any safer. There's a culture there that survives, thrives really, on drugs, sex, death, and murder. Unless Robert Pickton dies in custody, he's likely going to live long enough to be released (at the ripe age of 90). That fact is the most frightening in this case from my perspective because he's already made it very clear... when he gets out he's going right back to doing what he knows how to do best, murder innocent women.

Illustration 7: Homicide Det.
Chris Swinney

Chris Swinney, is an active Homicide Detective in the San Francisco Bay area. His writing includes the bestselling '*Bill Dix*

Detective Series' which he based the books on his experience as a cop.

Chris is a big time supporter of Teachers, Parents, Law Enforcement, Doctors, Nurses, Firefighters, American Troops, Juvenile Diabetes Research, and children. He spends time volunteering for his church, at schools, he coaches, and every once in awhile he gets to go fly fishing.

Visit Chris's page at:
rjparkerpublishing.com/c-l--swinney.html

Citations

1. Articles from the *Vancouver Sun* and *The Province*, 1998-2002.
2. http://criminalminds.wikia.com/wiki/Robert_Pickton
3. Greene, Trevor. "Bad Date: The Lost Girls of Vancouver's Low Track" (ECW Press, 2001).
4. *Toronto Star* (March 12, 2004). "'Outrage, anger, disgust' over pig farm meat scare."
5. http://www.cbc.ca/canada/british-columbia/story/2007/12/11/bc-picktonsentencing.html
6. Rod Mickleburgh (2010-08-04). "Pickton legal saga ends as remaining charges stayed."
7. "Pickton won't face remaining 20 murder charges." The Vancouver Sun. 2010-08-04.
8. "Horrors of Pickton trial revealed in graphic detail." National Post. 2007-02-20
9. http://www.cbc.ca/canada/british-columbia/story/2007/12/11/bc-picktonsentencing.html
10. "Death Farm." The Stranger. 2003-10-30.
11. http://www.thestar.com/news/2007/01/24/jury_gets_glimpse_of_picktons_mind.html

CPSIA information can be obtained
at www.ICGtesting.com
Printed in the USA
LVOW04s1927021016

506955LV00001B/31/P